FEMALE FIRSTS IN THEIR FIELDS

Air & Space

Broadcasting & Journalism

Business & Industry

Entertainment & Performing Arts

Government & Politics

Literature

Science & Medicine

Sports & Athletics

FEMALE FIRSTS IN THEIR FIELDS

GOVERNMENT & POLITICS

Veda Boyd Jones

Introduction by
Roslyn Rosen

CHELSEA HOUSE PUBLISHERS
Philadelphia

Produced by P. M. Gordon Associates, Inc.
Philadelphia, Pennsylvania

Editor in Chief Stephen Reginald
Managing Editor James D. Gallagher
Production Manager Pamela Loos
Art Director Sara Davis
Director of Photography Judy L. Hasday
Senior Production Editor Lisa Chippendale
Publishing Coordinator James McAvoy

Picture research by Gillian Speeth, Picture This
Cover illustration by Cliff Spohn
Cover design by Keith Trego

Frontispiece: Madeleine Albright

The Chelsea House World Wide Web site address is
http://www.chelseahouse.com

First Printing

1 3 5 7 9 8 6 4 2

Library of Congress Cataloging-in-Publication Data

Female Firsts in Their Fields. Government & politics / Veda Boyd Jones.
        p. cm.
    Includes bibliographical references and index.
    Summary: Profiles women who have been active in politics and govern-
ment, including Barbara Jordan, Gerldine Ferraro, and Sandra Day
O'Connor.
    ISBN 0-7910-5140-4 (hardcover)
    1. Women in politics–United States–Juvenile literature. [1. Women in
politics. 2. Women–Biography.] I. Title. II. Title: Government & politics.
III. Title: Government and politics.
HQ1236.5.U6J67 1998
320′.082–dc21
    [B]   98-45391
                                                                  CIP
                                                                   AC

CONTENTS

INTRODUCTION

Roslyn Rosen

When I was a toddler, it struck me that the other people in my family's New York apartment building were different. They did not use their hands when they talked, and they did not have to watch each other speak. I had been born deaf, and I felt sorry for them because they did not know the joy of drawing pictures in the air. They could not splash ideas into the air with a jab of the finger or a wave of the hand. Not until later did I realize the downside of being deaf–I couldn't communicate directly with my grandparents and extended family members, I depended on others to make important phone calls for me, and I found life's opportunities narrower, in part because I had few deaf (let alone female) role models.

Gallaudet University in Washington, D.C., is the only college for deaf students in the world. I arrived there in September 1958. It was a haven where sign language was part of the educational process, where there were deaf professors, and where opportunities for extracurricular leadership abounded. At Gallaudet I met deaf female professionals for the first time, although there were probably not more than three or four. The president and administrators of Gallaudet were all males who could hear–typical of school administrations during those years.

In my first month at Gallaudet, I also met the man who would become my husband. My destiny was charted: major in something that I could use as a homemaker (since that would be my job), get married, have a bunch of kids, and live happily ever after. This was the expectation for women in the late 1950s and early 1960s. And I stuck to the script: I majored in art with an emphasis on education and English, got married, and had three children. My life was complete—or so I thought.

The 1960s were turbulent and thought-provoking years. The civil rights movement and the beginnings of a women's movement emphasized human rights and equality for all. I came to see how alike the issues were that faced women, people of color, and people with disabilities, in terms of human rights and respect for human differences. Multicultural studies are vital for this understanding. Changes were occurring at an accelerating rate. Those changes affected my husband and me by broadening our traditional gender roles. With my husband's support, I pursued a master's degree in education of deaf students and later a doctoral degree in education administration. From my first job as a part-time sign language teacher, I eventually joined the faculty at Gallaudet University. In 1981 I was promoted to dean of the College for Continuing Education, and in 1993, to vice president for academic affairs.

During the formative years of my career, many of my role models and mentors were deaf men who had reached positions of leadership. They hired, taught, advised, and encouraged me. There were times when I felt the effects of the "glass ceiling" (an invisible barrier that keeps women or minorities from rising any higher). Sometimes I needed to depend on my male colleagues because my access to "old boy" networks or decision makers was limited. When I became involved with the National Association of the Deaf (NAD), the world's oldest organization of deaf people, I met deaf women who became role models—Dr. Gertie Galloway was the first deaf female president of the NAD, and Marcella Meyer had founded the Greater Los Angeles Community Service of the Deaf (GLAD). In 1980 I was elected to the board of directors of the National Association of the Deaf, and in 1990, I became the second woman elected president of NAD.

When I became a dean at Gallaudet in 1981, I also became a member of the school's Council of Deans, which at the time included only two deaf deans and two female deans. I was the only deaf woman dean. The vice president was a white male, and he once commented that top administrators often build management teams in their own image. I have found that to be true. As a dean, I was the highest-ranking deaf woman at Gallaudet, and I was able to hire and help a number of young deaf female professionals within the College for Continuing Education and our regional centers around the country. In the five years that I have been vice president at Gallaudet I have added many deaf, female, and minority members to my own management team. When I was the president of NAD, I hired its first deaf female executive director, Nancy Bloch. I also encouraged two of my friends, Mabs Holcomb and Sharon Wood, to write the first deaf women history book, a source of inspiration for young deaf girls.

It is important for women who have reached the top levels of their fields to advise and help younger women to become successful. It is also important for young girls to know about the groundbreaking contributions of women who came before them. The women profiled in this series of biographies overcame many obstacles to succeed. Some had physical handicaps, others fought generations of discriminatory attitudes toward women in the workplace. The world may never provide equal opportunities for every human being, but we can all work together to improve life for the next generation.

DR. ROSLYN ROSEN is the Vice President for Academic Affairs at Gallaudet University in Washington, D.C. Dr. Rosen has served as a board member and President of the National Association of the Deaf (NAD), the oldest consumer organization in the world, and was a member of the National Captioning Institute's executive board for nine years. She is currently a board member of the World Federation of the Deaf. Dr. Rosen also wears the hats of daughter, wife, mother, and proud grandmother.

BARBARA JORDAN

Her deep voice rolled like thunder across the nation. "My faith in the Con-sti-tu-tion is whole. It is com-plete. It is to-tal."

On a hot July night in 1974, millions of Americans had turned on their televisions to view the hearings on President Richard Nixon's impeachment. Each member of the Judiciary Committee of the House of Representatives was to speak on whether charges should be brought against the president to remove him from office.

Who would have expected that the first black woman from the South elected to Congress would stir the nation with her eloquent words?

Barbara Jordan defended the Constitution that, when it was written in 1787, had not even included her. "I felt for many years that somehow George Washington and Alexander Hamilton just left me out by mistake. But through the process of amendment, interpretation, and court decision, I have finally been included in 'We the people.' "

Jordan had carefully researched impeachment. That July

Barbara Jordan argues for the proposed Equal Rights Amendment before a U.S. House subcommittee.

11

night, she explained why she believed the president should be removed from office for obstructing justice and covering up the criminal activities of others. Her message was clear, logical, and based on law.

The next day, a man in her hometown of Houston, Texas, put up 25 billboards that said: "Thank You, Barbara Jordan, for Explaining the Constitution to Us."

She received thousands of letters from citizens—young and old, black and white, from the North and South and East and West—praising her for her wonderful speech. This large black woman, 38 years old and in her first term in Congress, had made the nation sit up and take notice.

It had not always been that way.

Barbara Charline Jordan was born February 21, 1936, in Houston, Texas, the third daughter of Arlyne and Benjamin Jordan. She grew up in a brick house in the Fifth Ward, one of the few black sections of town that had indoor plumbing, electricity, and paved streets. Her father's father and stepmother lived with them in their two-bedroom home. The three girls shared a fold-out bed in the dining room.

Although she was brought up in a strict Baptist home, Barbara's religious training came from her mother's father, John Ed Patten. He was not a churchgoing man like her other relatives, but he taught her how to live. She was not to trust the world; she should figure things out for herself; but she should love humanity anyway. He made her recite: "Just remember the world is not a playground, but a schoolroom. Life is not a holiday but an education. One eternal lesson for us all: to teach us how better we should love."

Barbara helped Grandpa Patten with his junkyard business. She sorted newspapers, scrap metal, and rags for a share of the profits. While they worked together, he shared his philosophy of life. His fierce independence rubbed off on her. "You just trot your own horse and don't get into the same rut as everyone else," he told her. She never forgot his words.

When Barbara turned 13, her father felt called to the ministry, so he added that work to his regular job at the Houston Terminal Warehouse and Cold Storage Company. He moved his family into their own home on Campbell Street in a very poor black neighborhood, but the family took pride in home ownership and kept their house painted pink and their yard neatly mowed. Barbara's father had high standards for himself, and he expected nothing less of his three daughters. His plans for them included a college education.

Barbara excelled at Phillis Wheatley High School. After a woman attorney spoke at her school her sophomore year, Barbara decided to be a lawyer. She joined the debate team, a natural for her. Her voice–deep, strong, and powerful–made people listen. She won nearly every speech contest she entered, including the National Ushers Oratorical Contest, where she spoke on the importance of an education. When interviewed for a black newspaper after her return from Chicago with the first prize of a $200 scholarship, she said, "It's just another milestone I have passed; it's just the beginning."

But it would be an uphill fight. The civil rights movement had begun, but integration would move slowly. Barbara's world was a black one. Her experience with whites was limited. After graduation from her all-black high school in 1952, she attended the relatively new all-black Texas Southern University in Houston. Again on the debate team, she traveled into other states to other colleges and encountered restaurants that wouldn't serve blacks and service stations that wouldn't allow blacks to use the restrooms.

After graduation from TSU, Barbara traveled to the East. What a different world she found at Boston University Law School! Of the other students in her class, 5 were women (one was black) and 592 were white men. Most of them had worked at law offices in the summer. They knew the vocabulary of *torts* and *lessees* and *promisors*. They had gone to schools that had prepared them to study law.

Barbara Jordan learned that her segregated education had not been "separate but equal," as some lawmakers had claimed for years. Her black education was inferior; she had not been taught to think and reason and defend her positions.

"I felt that in order to compensate for what I had missed in earlier years, I would have to work harder, and study longer, than anyone else." She studied until the wee hours of the morning and rarely got more than four hours of sleep a night during those three years at law school.

But it was worth it. In 1959 she graduated from law school and took the bar exam in Massachusetts for an attorney's license. In the fall, she returned to Texas and passed the bar exam there, too.

With printed cards that read "Barbara Jordan, Attorney at Law," she set up an office in her parents' dining room. Business was slow in the beginning, so Barbara volunteered her time to work for the Harris County Democrats. She stuffed envelopes and licked stamps for the John Kennedy–Lyndon Johnson campaign. One evening she substituted for a speaker who was ill and found that crowds liked her forceful manner of oratory, just as they had years earlier in her high school and college days. She liked politics, and it seemed to like her.

She moved her office downtown with another

young lawyer and decided to run for the Texas House of Representatives. In 1962, she borrowed the $500 necessary to file for election. She studied a thick book on Texas government, campaigned on reform throughout the district, but was disappointed on Election Day. She earned 46,000 votes, but white lawyer Willis Whatley got 65,000.

In 1964, she ran again and lost. Now she stopped and asked herself what she should do. She loved politics, but "I did not like losing. I intended to devote my full attention to figuring out the way to succeed."

The Supreme Court stepped in and helped her out. It required legislative districts to be based on a region's population and not drawn along county lines. This affirmed the constitutional principle of every person's vote being equal. In 1965, Texas had to reshape its legislative districts, and Barbara Jordan lived in the new 11th State Senatorial District. People in this area had supported her before. Why not try her luck again, this time for state senator in the 1966 election?

Her opponent, Charles Whitfield, had already served eight years in the senate. He campaigned on a race issue, urging black people not to vote for Jordan just because she was black. "Can a white man win?" became his campaign slogan. Jordan picked up his cry, and in her thunderous voice she ended most of her speeches: "My opponent asks, 'Can a white man win?' And I say to you: 'No. Not this time. Not . . . this . . . time!' " That response brought crowds to their feet.

Barbara Jordan won a resounding victory and became the first black woman in the Texas legislature. She did not take the senate by storm when she was sworn in. She worked her way in, little by little. She studied each issue that was brought before

Jordan celebrates after winning the 1966 Democratic nomination for the Texas Senate.

*In 1972 Jordan (center)
became the first black woman
from the South to be elected
to the U.S. House of
Representatives.*

the senate, so she could base her voting decision on fact and law.

She'd been a senator for only a month when President Lyndon B. Johnson asked select civil rights leaders to the White House to preview his fair-housing bill. He included her on the invitation list. Of course, Jordan accepted. Her presence there made the newspapers, and the *Washington Post* called her "a practical politician who understands reality." That was the basis for her solid friendship with Johnson, also a Texas Democrat, who was a practical man.

Back in Austin, Senator Jordan continued to learn the rules of legislating, both the written ones and the ones not in the books. She made educated decisions and chose her positions carefully. When she spoke on the senate floor, she commanded attention. Her colleagues voted her Outstanding Freshman Senator at the end of the legislative session. In 1968 her proud constituents reelected her to a four-year term.

After the 1970 census, a new U.S. congressional district was formed because of an increase in the Texas population. Many of the voters in this new district were the ones who had sent Jordan to the state senate. Once again, Jordan looked at redistricting and saw an opportunity. She threw her hat in the ring for the U.S. House of Representatives. At a campaign fund-raising event, former President Johnson called her "a woman of keen intellect and unusual legislative ability."

In May 1972, Jordan easily won the Democratic primary with 80 percent of the votes. While awaiting the November election, she finished out her term in the state senate, where her colleagues had elected her president pro tem. Texas tradition demands that the governor and lieutenant governor leave the state for a day so that the president pro tem can be acting governor. Barbara Jordan's day was set for June 10. Her family, including her ailing father, traveled to Austin for the festivities. Later that day, her father suffered a stroke, but he had seen his daughter sworn in as the first black woman governor in the country. He died the following morning.

The November election was an easy victory for Jordan. She headed to Washington and secured an appointment to the Judiciary Committee. Her stirring speech on the Constitution the night of the impeachment hearings in 1974 catapulted her to national attention.

Jordan wanted to be on the committee to present the indictment of President Nixon to the Senate, but he resigned before that could happen. A month later, the new president, Gerald Ford, asked Jordan to go to China with a group including Senator William Fulbright and Senator Hubert Humphrey to continue Nixon's foreign policy. Good company, Jordan thought, so she agreed to go.

One night in China, Jordan received a phone call. A reporter from a Houston newspaper wanted her reaction to Ford's pardon of Nixon. She was stunned. Had Ford sent her group out of the country so they wouldn't be around when he dismissed all charges against Nixon? She felt the country had been cheated of a trial, but that was the end of the impeachment ordeal.

Jordan was reelected to Congress in 1974. She continued to study legislation and spent 14-hour days on the job—if not on the floor of Congress, in the library, or in her office. She was rather surprised

Jordan delivers her keynote speech at the 1992 Democratic convention.

when she received a call from Bob Strauss, the Democratic National Committee chairman, asking her to give a keynote address at the 1976 Democratic National Convention along with former astronaut John Glenn. She agreed.

Glenn spoke first. As usual, delegates milled about and talked loud enough to drown out the speaker. That was the normal way. Speakers were to focus on the TV audience. Barbara Jordan was nervous, but when her turn to speak came, she began in her booming voice. In moments, the great convention hall was as quiet as a church. Delegates were mesmerized by the speech given by the first black woman ever to speak to a Democratic convention. She spoke of equality for all and privileges for none, and when she finished, the crowd went wild.

"We want Barbara!" they chanted. They clapped

their hands, stomped their feet, and waved their banners.

Barbara Jordan, the great orator, had done it again—set America talking about what was good in the country. She easily won reelection that year, which was her final election.

In 1979 she retired from public life. It is likely she knew then that she was suffering from multiple sclerosis. But deteriorating health didn't stop her from beginning a new career teaching at the University of Texas at the Lyndon Baines Johnson School of Public Affairs. Her classes were so popular, a drawing was held each semester to see who could be her students.

Occasionally she would step back into the national spotlight—giving the keynote speech at the 1992 Democratic convention and chairing the 1995 Commission for Immigration Reform. Each time, the voice of Barbara Jordan resonated across the nation.

She died on January 17, 1996, of pneumonia.

Feminist Gloria Steinem said of Barbara Jordan, "It's hard to imagine anyone not treating her with respect. I was in awe of her. She was someone in whose presence all thoughts of racial and sexual biases evaporated."

SANDRA DAY O'CONNOR 2

W hen Arizona judge Sandra Day O'Connor answered the phone one day in July 1981, on the other end of the line was Warren Burger, Chief Justice of the Supreme Court. He told her that she had been selected to fill a vacancy on the high court. Moments into their conversation, O'Connor put him on hold. She had another call.

On the other line, President Ronald Reagan offered her the position as the first woman justice on the Supreme Court. Of course, she said yes.

That yes was merely the first step on O'Connor's climb to the highest court in the nation. The Senate Judiciary Committee had to approve her appointment, and the entire Senate had to vote on whether she was mentally strong enough, smart enough, and wise enough to interpret the laws of the land.

She was all those things—and more.

Sandra Day was born March 26, 1930, in El Paso, Texas, the first child of Harry and Ada Mae Day. She grew up on the giant Lazy B Ranch, which sprawled over 185,000 acres in Arizona and New Mexico. Her home at that time had only

Supreme Court Justice Sandra Day O'Connor in the early 1990s.

four rooms, no running water, and no electricity. Four cowhands bunked on the screened-in front porch.

The isolation of the ranch was not a hardship for Sandra. She found companionship in the cats in the barnyard, swam in the stock watering tank, and read books and magazines. Her mother, who had earned a college degree at a time when few women attended college, taught her to read by the time she was four.

The nearest school was many miles away, so when she was six, Sandra moved to El Paso to stay with her grandmother, Mamie Wilkey. She attended the Radford School for Girls, but longed for the summer months when she lived at the ranch.

She tackled life with both hands and practiced skills until she could do everything well. By the time she was eight, she could drive a pickup, brand cattle, fix windmills, mend fences, ride a horse, and shoot a .22 rifle with accuracy.

After her sister, Ann, and her brother, Alan, were born, Sandra found it even harder to leave home for the school term. She convinced her parents to let her attend a school in Lordsburg, New Mexico, for a year, but the commute proved difficult. Back she went to El Paso and to her grandmother, a very influential woman.

"She was a wonderful person—very supportive of me," Sandra later said. "She would always tell me that I could do anything I wanted to do. She was convinced of that, and it was very encouraging."

Sandra skipped a grade at Radford and graduated from Austin High School at the age of 16. She attended college at prestigious Stanford University in California. Her college roommate, Marilyn Brown, later said about Sandra, "Even though she was younger than us, she always seemed to handle it.

She never got upset. She never went into a panic about anything. And she was fun."

As with every challenge in her life, Sandra tackled college with determination. "I think that anything you do in life requires preparation," she later said. She studied hard for classes and still had time to take friends home to the ranch during school breaks. By the time she graduated with high honors, she was already taking classes at Stanford Law School.

One day while working on the *Stanford Law Review,* a journal edited by students, she met John Jay O'Connor III. He took her out to dinner that night, which was the beginning of a long courtship. Six months after she graduated from law school third in her class, Sandra married John, who was in the law class behind her.

While her husband finished his last semester in law school, Sandra Day O'Connor searched for a job. Even though she had excelled in school, law firm after law firm turned down her application. They weren't prepared to hire a female attorney. One firm offered her a job as a legal secretary, but she declined. Instead of joining a private law firm, she looked at public service and went to work as a law clerk in the office of the San Mateo, California, county attorney. Soon she was promoted to deputy county attorney.

When John was drafted in 1953 for the Korean conflict, she accompanied him to his post in Frankfurt, West Germany. He served in the army's legal division, while she worked as a civilian lawyer for the Quartermaster Corps, checking military contracts. During the three years they lived abroad, they traveled to 14 countries and skied the mountains of Europe.

In December 1956, the O'Connors returned to

the United States. They built a house in Phoenix, Arizona, and both passed the bar exam, which allowed them to practice law in that state. John O'Connor quickly joined a law firm, but in October 1957 Sandra O'Connor gave birth to her first son, Scott. She wanted to stay in the legal profession, so she opened an office with another attorney and worked only mornings. That way she could spend most of her day with Scott. When her second son, Brian, was born in 1960, she decided to stop practicing law for a while to raise her family. A couple of years later, her third son, Jay, was born.

While she was home caring for her family, she became involved in community activities and volunteered to work for the Republican party. Even when she decided to reenter the legal profession in 1965, she continued her community activism. Her part-time work as a state assistant attorney general stretched to more and more hours as her sons grew older. Soon she was back to full-time work.

In 1969, when a vacancy occurred in Sandra O'Connor's senatorial district, the Republican governor appointed her to the position. She filled out the term and then won the seat in the next election, calling herself conservative in financial matters but overall "a moderate Republican." Two years later, she was reelected. When Republican senators met to elect a majority leader, who would organize committees and coordinate bills, they decided on O'Connor. She was the first woman to serve as majority leader in the senate of any state in the country.

As she had done all her life, O'Connor tackled her legislative career by being prepared. She read volumes on each issue and was ready for every discussion on the senate floor. She looked at issues from both sides and turned them around and looked at them again. She was considered a "middle-roader," not too conservative and not too liberal, and worked hard to make laws reflect common sense.

Near the end of her second full term, Senator O'Connor decided it was time to choose between law and politics. Law won. She ran for trial judge on the Maricopa County Superior Court. She defeated the judge who was running for reelection and became known for her hard stand against crime. Every time she entered her courtroom, she had read the files of the cases and had reviewed the laws that would apply to them. She did not like wasting time any more than she liked lawyers who were unprepared. She ran her courtroom in a fair and just manner.

In 1979, O'Connor was appointed to the Arizona Court of Appeals by Governor Bruce Babbitt, who said, "Her intellectual ability and her judgment are astounding." On this court, she sat with two other judges and ruled on law and principle. Instead of trials by juries, these judges listened to lawyers argue cases; then the judges discussed the cases and voted. One of the judges in the voting majority would write an opinion that stated their decision on the case and the reasons for it. A judge who agreed, but differed on the reasoning, could submit a concurring opinion. A judge who disagreed could write a dissenting opinion to express an opposite view.

Two years after her appointment to the appellate court, President Reagan nominated Sandra Day O'Connor to the Supreme Court, calling her "a person for all seasons." Following a round of courtesy calls to members of Congress and senators on Capitol Hill in Washington, D.C., O'Connor prepared for a grilling by the Senate Judiciary Committee. She had opponents in the public sector, most notably the anti-abortion groups, because she had made some concessions to abortion legislation when she

Fundamentalist preacher Carl McIntire leads a demonstration against O'Connor's nomination to the Supreme Court. Conservatives disliked her record on abortion rights.

was a state senator. When asked about the abortion issue by the committee, she sidestepped answering. She said she should not discuss something that could come before the Court and might be better handled by lawmakers.

"I know well the difference between a legislator and a judge," she said, "and the role of the judge is to interpret the law, not make it."

She passed the committee hearings by a vote of 17–0. A week later, the entire Senate voted on her nomination. She waited in an anteroom after the five-minute buzzer called the senators to vote.

"This is the longest five minutes of my life," she said and wrung her hands.

She need not have been nervous. The Senate confirmed her appointment by a vote of 99–0, since one senator was absent. As she stood on the Capitol steps afterward, she looked across at the Supreme Court building and said, "My hope is that ten years from now, after I've been across the street and worked for awhile, they'll feel glad that they gave me this wonderful vote."

On September 25, 1981, Sandra Day O'Connor, 51 years old, was sworn in as the 102nd member of the Supreme Court and the first woman justice.

The Supreme Court is in session from October to June. Each year some 5,000 petitioners want their cases heard, but the Court can only hear approximately 150. Its first business is to choose which cases should be heard, which takes considerable time.

Two weeks during most months, the Court hears oral arguments from lawyers, much like the Arizona Court of Appeals where Justice O'Connor served earlier. The nine justices vote on a case, and one member writes the majority opinion. O'Connor has distinguished herself by her clear and concise writing style. Sometimes she writes a dissenting opin-

In September 1981 O'Connor is sworn in as the first woman justice of the Supreme Court. As Chief Justice Warren Burger administers the oath, O'Connor places her hand on two family Bibles held by her husband, John J. O'Connor.

ion, when she votes against the majority and wants her views known.

She puts in 12-hour work days. When in 1988 she was diagnosed with breast cancer, she didn't let it slow her down. She spoke at a college, a 3½ hour journey from her home, the night before her surgery. She scheduled chemotherapy on Fridays so she could be at work on Monday mornings. After all her treatments were completed, doctors gave her a clean bill of health.

O'Connor can see many sides of a situation and understands the Constitution. She may agree with liberals on one issue and conservatives on the next, and she bridges the gap between the two. She sees each case individually and is fair and impartial as she evaluates it.

In her childhood on the ranch, Sandra Day mended fences. With her immense negotiating skills, Justice Sandra Day O'Connor is still mending fences, but now between opposing views.

GERALDINE FERRARO

3

"Gerr-eee! Gerr-eee!" Delegates at the 1984 Democratic National Convention in San Francisco, California, chanted her name, clapped their hands, and stomped their feet. The roar was deafening as Congresswoman Geraldine Ferraro of Queens, New York, walked onto the stage to accept the nomination as the party's first woman vice presidential candidate.

"By choosing an American woman to run for our nation's second-highest office, you send a powerful signal to all Americans," she told the crowd. "There are no doors we cannot unlock. We will place no limits on achievement. If we can do this, we can do *anything*."

She had always believed that America was the land where doors would open if a person worked hard and earned the right to enter. That creed had worked for her time and again.

Geraldine Anne Ferraro was born August 26, 1935, in Newburgh, New York, the fourth child and only daughter of Dominick and Antonetta Ferraro. Her older brother's twin

---

Campaigning for the vice presidency in 1984, Ferraro holds up a T-shirt with the message "A Woman's Place Is in the White House."

had died six days after his birth. Her brother Gerard, while sitting on his mother's lap, had died in a car crash when he was three. Her mother had become so despondent, the doctor recommended that she have another child. That child was Geraldine, who was named after her dead brother.

Her father, an Italian immigrant, owned a restaurant and dime store. He was the hero of Gerry's young life. When he died of a heart attack when she was eight, she was devastated. Doctors said she held her grief inside, and she became ill with anemia for most of a year, too ill even to attend school.

Gerry's mother was left with little money when her husband died. She moved her son and daughter to the South Bronx and took a job in the garment industry, sewing beads on dresses. She was determined to make a better life for her children, and she believed the way was through education.

"My father's death changed my life forever," Geraldine has said since. "I found out how quickly what you have can be taken away. From that moment on, I had to fight for whatever I wanted, to work and study my own way out of the South Bronx and take my mother with me. For every plan I made, I made sure I had an alternative to fall back on. I had learned that the hard way–and so had my mother."

Gerry's mother scrimped and saved and managed to send Gerry to boarding school in Tarrytown, New York, on partial scholarship. At Marymount School Gerry skipped a couple of grades and graduated at 16. She secured a full scholarship to Marymount College in Manhattan and earned a bachelor of arts degree in English in 1956. At the same time, she studied education at Hunter College. For four years Gerry taught elementary school in Queens, where her mother now lived. Again with financial help from her mother, Gerry continued her education at

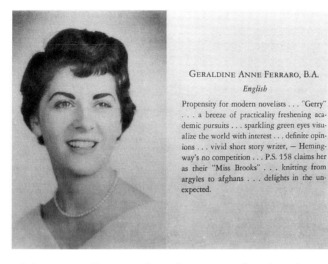

GERALDINE ANNE FERRARO, B.A.

English

Propensity for modern novelists . . . "Gerry" . . . a breeze of practicality freshening academic pursuits . . . sparkling green eyes visualize the world with interest . . . definite opinions . . . vivid short story writer, — Hemingway's no competition . . . P.S. 158 claims her as their "Miss Brooks" . . . knitting from argyles to afghans . . . delights in the unexpected.

Ferraro's entry in the 1956 yearbook of Marymount College in Manhattan.

night at Fordham University Law School and graduated with a law degree. She passed the bar exam in July 1960, and soon afterward she married real estate developer John Zaccaro.

As a tribute to her mother, she kept Ferraro as her professional name after her marriage. Her mother had always said, "Don't forget your name. *Ferro* means 'iron.' You can bend it, but you can't break it."

Years later when speaking at Marymount University at the end of the vice presidential campaign, Geraldine Ferraro stressed that her education had been invaluable in making her life choices. And she owed her education to her mother. "Because of her sacrifice, I had the privilege to attend this college. Because of that dedication, I am what I am today. And tonight, I would like to say to her from the bottom of my heart: Thank you for everything." She turned to face her mother, who sat in the audience. "I hope you are proud of me. I will always be proud of you."

After her marriage, Geraldine Ferraro spent the next 14 years at home, raising three children, Donna,

John Jr., and Laura. Ferraro volunteered for the Democratic Party, and occasionally she worked part-time for her husband's real estate business. It wasn't until her youngest daughter was in second grade that she practiced law full-time as an assistant district attorney in Queens.

Ferraro helped create the Special Victims Bureau and two years later was appointed bureau chief. Her work with victims of violent crimes was emotionally draining and professionally demanding. She earned a reputation as a tough prosecutor, but as a result of facing criminals and victims, she changed her political philosophy from fairly conservative to liberal. She believed that at the root of the problems she saw lay poverty and social injustices. She couldn't change those things in the prosecutor's office, so in 1978 she turned to politics.

What she didn't know about the political arena, she figured she could learn. "'How are you ever going to do it?' I had wondered every time I launched myself on a new course. But I found out. You work hard, you prepare, you give it your all, and within a short time you're on top of it."

She ran for Congress in the Ninth District of Queens, a melting pot of nationalities, and she landed on top. Now could she start solving the problems that kept people poor and made children criminals?

With a motto of "We're Here to Help" printed at the top of her congressional newsletter, she set up a storefront office in Queens to serve the people of her district. She worked hard, reading legislation, studying issues, and meeting key people on the floor of the House of Representatives, yet she kept her family first in her life. She spent long weekends in Queens with her family and lived in Washington, D.C., during the week while Congress was in session.

Ferraro appears with Walter Mondale in July 1984 after the announcement that she will be his running mate—the first woman candidate for the vice presidency.

She built quite a reputation as a spunky woman in the House. Although she kept a cheerful down-to-earth manner, she stuck up for what she believed in a forthright, effective way. She easily won reelection in 1980 and 1982.

Ferraro moved into the national spotlight as chair of the Platform Committee for the 1984 Democratic Convention. She held hearings across the country, gathering the opinions of citizens, to decide what stand the Democratic Party would take on issues facing the nation, and she met more and more Democrats.

Her name was not yet a household word, but it was on former Vice President Walter Mondale's list of finalists for his running mate. He had captured enough delegates to win the Democratic nomina-

During the grueling 1984 campaign, Ferraro responds to critics of her family's finances.

tion for president, but he needed a vice presidential candidate who could help him beat Republican incumbents President Ronald Reagan and Vice President George Bush.

Mondale interviewed several possible candidates and decided on Ferraro. He later said she had "worked hard for everything she's achieved. She has a strong family life, deep religious convictions," and she knew the struggles and dreams of average Americans. He offered her the vice presidential slot on the Democratic ticket, and she accepted.

Across the country, the historic selection of a woman as a vice presidential candidate met with mixed reactions. Some people felt that a woman wouldn't be capable of running the government. After all, the vice president was only a presidential heartbeat away from becoming president. Could a woman who didn't have military experience be commander-in-chief, if she had to? Ferraro was adamant in her stance. If she were president, she said, "quite frankly, I'm prepared to do whatever is necessary in order to secure this country and make sure that security is maintained."

Other people didn't question her ability, and women across the nation celebrated the victory of a woman going where no other woman had gone. Ann Richards, then state treasurer of Texas and later governor, said of Ferraro's nomination, "The first thing I thought of was not winning in the political sense, but of my two daughters. To think of the numbers of young women who can now aspire to anything!"

Geraldine Ferraro wasn't running for vice president just for herself; she represented women everywhere. "She's the universal woman," Connecticut Congress member Barbara Kennelly said. "She passes all the tests."

And there were lots of tests. The media focused a microscope on her life and her family's life. They questioned her husband's finances, her dead father's honesty, and her religious beliefs, because of her pro-choice stand on abortion. She even received threats on her life. When the long four-month campaign was over, she was exhausted. She had crisscrossed the country several times, spoken to hundreds of groups, and shaken thousands of hands.

The Mondale-Ferraro ticket was soundly defeated, but women everywhere had won because of her candidacy. Was the grueling campaign worth it? Absolutely. Young women had seen another barrier broken down and the boundaries for their futures widened.

After the election, Ferraro started a political action committee, Americans Concerned for Tomorrow, that donated money directly to women candidates. In 1992, she ran in the Democratic primary for Senate and was defeated. Since then she has practiced law with a New York law firm, and for several years she appeared on Cable News Network's *Crossfire,* where she debated conservative John Sununu, who was President Bush's chief of staff. At the end of each program, she signed off, "From the left," emphasizing her liberal stand on social programs.

In January 1998 she ran for senator from New York and lost, but she remains a liberal voice in America and continues to work to open doors for others.

CAROL MOSELEY-BRAUN

4

When the brand-new freshman senator from Illinois visited the Senate chamber for the first time, she wandered the aisle until she found her seat. Over a century before it had belonged to Abraham Lincoln's debating opponent Stephen A. Douglas.

"In the days when Douglas sat there, someone like me was considered a nonperson," Carol Moseley-Braun said, as she prepared to become the first black woman to ever serve in the U.S. Senate. "I feel blessed to be an agent of change. My victory represents a turning of the corner for our country."

It had been a slow, step-by-step walk to reach that corner.

Carol Elizabeth Moseley was born on August 16, 1947, in Chicago, to Joseph and Edna Moseley. She was the oldest of four children. Because of her dad's dream of being a jazz musician, their home embraced a multiracial world of musicians from multicultural backgrounds. The family called their home the "United Nations of 41st Street." Prejudice was entirely foreign to that house.

Carol Moseley-Braun celebrates her 1992 election to the U.S. Senate, where she would occupy the seat once held by Stephen A. Douglas.

Carol's mother was a medical technician, and she told her daughter, "You can do anything." She taught her children a poem which they repeated often:

When a job is once begun,
Never stop until it's done.
Be the job large or small,
Do it right or not at all.

Carol's father was a policeman who didn't know how to control his own violence. He abused his family, and when her mother would withdraw inside herself, Carol would be left to defend her younger brothers and sister as her father beat them with a rope.

When Carol was 15, her parents finally divorced. Her mother took Carol and her brothers and sister to live with their grandmother in a slum neighborhood nicknamed "Bucket of Blood" because of the violence on its streets. Seeing the utter hopelessness around her made Carol want to improve society.

During her days at Parker High School, Carol became a civil rights activist. She staged a one-person sit-in at a restaurant where she had been denied service because she was black. She endured stones thrown at her when she spread her towel on a previously all-white beach. And she walked with Martin Luther King Jr. in a march for open housing. His composure, while insults and threats rained on him from all sides, kept her from striking back at the mob and taught her that nonviolence was a way to get things done.

She attended the University of Illinois at Chicago and graduated in 1969 with a degree in political science. Three years later she graduated from the University of Chicago Law School. The following year, she married Michael Braun, an attorney whom she'd met while they were both in school.

Moseley-Braun worked as an assistant U.S. attorney until her son Matthew's birth in 1977. A year later she entered politics with a run for the state legislature and won, keeping that seat until 1988. For one year (1983) she served as assistant majority leader in the Illinois House of Representatives. She was the first woman and the first black to fill that post.

As a legislator, Moseley-Braun delighted in tough debates over welfare, gun control, education, and health care. To diffuse anger at the end of a debate, she usually shook her opponents' hands and sometimes gave them fanciful T-shirts or balloons.

"Carol is not your usual politician," commented fellow state representative Mary Flowers.

The year 1986 proved a hard one for Moseley-Braun. Her interracial marriage ended in divorce, leaving her a single mother. Her own mother, who had ten years earlier suffered a stroke, had a leg amputated and was confined to a wheelchair. Moseley-Braun's brother Johnny, who suffered from manic-depression, died of drug and alcohol abuse. With all these traumatic events, she had hoped for a ray of sunshine in her life—to be named to the Democratic ticket as candidate for lieutenant governor—but she was disappointed.

It wasn't until 1988 that she ran for a different office, recorder of deeds for Cook County. With that victory, she became the first black elected to an executive office in the county.

But that wasn't enough for Moseley-Braun. She had always considered herself someone who didn't sit around but instead tried to bring about positive changes. That philosophy had prompted her activism in high school, and in 1991, it made her think about what she was seeing on television.

Women had brought charges of sexual harassment

A winning team: At a rally in October 1992, Moseley-Braun receives the support of her party's national standard-bearers, Bill Clinton and Al Gore.

against Judge Clarence Thomas during his Senate Judiciary Committee confirmation hearings as a Supreme Court justice. Professor Anita Hill testified against Thomas, and the committee questioned her over and over, often asking very personal questions. Moseley-Braun was angered by the behavior of the senators. She called the Senate "an elitist club made up of mostly white male millionaires over 50." She wasn't the only one angry. When Illinois senator Alan Dixon, who was on the committee, voted to confirm Thomas, other Illinois citizens started a "Draft Moseley-Braun" movement.

"By the time I got a letter from a white man in a Republican county urging me to run, I knew there was something up and I really ought to consider this seriously," Moseley-Braun said about the citizens' campaign.

Carol Moseley-Braun sat down at dinner with her son, Matthew, who was 15 at the time, and asked him what he thought about her running. After all, her decision would affect his life too. He asked her questions about her platform and told her that she should run, since her generation had left the world worse off than they had found it. His reasoning stunned her, and she considered what he'd said.

"And every time I would point out something that we had done that was positive and good, he would come back with something that was messed up. And the more he talked, the more it occurred to me that if I'm going to be in government, then I ought to try to make a contribution, I ought to try to be relevant,

I ought to try to make a difference. And so I decided at that point to go for it."

With little money in her election fund, Moseley-Braun threw her hat in the Democratic primary election ring against incumbent senator Alan Dixon and multimillionaire Al Hofeld. The two men raised huge campaign funds and spent dollars mostly on TV time lambasting each other. They ignored Moseley-Braun as no threat. Her campaign was disorganized, understaffed, and scrambling for advertising money, but it held together long enough to get her elected in an upset victory in March 1992.

Although some said the three-way race allowed Moseley-Braun to win with 38.9 percent of the vote, she dismissed that notion. "People are ready for a change. That's why I won."

Her campaign was tainted by a hint of scandal concerning money that Moseley-Braun's mother should have paid to Medicaid but gave to her children instead. The candidate said there was no impropriety, yet she paid the money to the government from her own funds.

With the weight of the Democratic Party now behind her, Moseley-Braun won the general election in November and became the first black woman in the U.S. Senate. She inserted a hyphen between her maiden name and her former husband's name so she wouldn't be called Senator Braun.

After the election, Moseley-Braun was criticized for taking a four-week vacation to Africa with her campaign manager and her son instead of reviewing issues for the upcoming Senate session as other freshmen senators were doing. As soon as she returned, she faced an aggressive press corps asking for answers to difficult questions—they wanted to know about her campaign debt and about allegations of sexual harassment against her campaign manager.

A few months after taking her seat in the U.S. Senate, Moseley-Braun throws the ceremonial first pitch for the Chicago White Sox at the team's home opener.

Making her voice heard: Moseley-Braun talks with her peers, influential Democratic senators Paul Simon (left) and Patrick Leahy. In the background are Senators Daniel Patrick Moynihan and Claiborne Pell.

"If this is a honeymoon, I'm going to divorce," she said of her first week in the nation's capital.

Now she had arrived. But what would she do as a senator?

Her first major challenge came when, as a member of the Judiciary Committee, she helped keep the United Daughters of the Confederacy from renewing their patent on their insignia. The insignia prominently displayed the Confederate flag, and Moseley-Braun was offended by it. She was furious on discovering that Senator Jesse Helms had sneaked the patent renewal into a larger bill that had been passed by the Senate. She stood before the senators and in an impassioned voice asked them to reconsider their vote. They listened, and enough reversed their votes so the patent was not renewed.

Even though Moseley-Braun's term was fraught with controversy, because she ran her office in her own distinctive manner, she believed she could make a difference. That's a message that she'd like Americans to understand. "It's most important to show people that they can have an impact. The evidence is there if they would just see it: that by engaging yourself in the affairs of your community, you can become a voice."

JANET RENO

With a Paul Bunyan stride, the tall, plain woman stepped behind the podium in the cobbled courtyard of the Justice Department. The April 6, 1993, afternoon in Washington, D.C., was chilly, but America's first woman attorney general faced a thousand of her employees in a lightweight suit. Janet Reno from Florida didn't own a topcoat. Buying one would have to go on her list of things to do in the nation's capital.

"I'm the new kid on the block, and I thought I should let you know my hopes and dreams and how I do things," she said. "While I'm the attorney general, we will address each issue with one question: What's the right thing to do?"

Janet Reno has lived her life by answering that question.

Janet's father, Henry Rasmussen, came to America from Denmark with his family when he was eleven. To avoid prejudice, her grandfather changed the family name to Reno by choosing the name from a map of the United States. As an adult, Henry Reno became a police reporter for the *Miami Herald* and retired from that job after 43 years.

Attorney General Janet Reno speaks to reporters at a press conference in 1998.

Janet's mother, Jane Wood, was also a journalist. Proclaimed a genius at an early age, she fought the tag and labeled herself simply her own person.

After Henry and Jane married, they had four children in quick succession. Janet was born July 21, 1938, followed by Robert, Margaret, and Mark. Their small house in Miami's Coconut Grove neighborhood was too confining, and in 1947 the Renos fled westward and bought 21 acres on the edge of the Everglades. They lived in a small frame house on the corner of the property until Jane Reno declared she was going to build them a new house. She read books and talked to a brick mason, an electrician, and a plumber about how to build it. She dug the foundation with a pick and a shovel, and two years later the rustic cypress-beamed home was ready for the family. Dubbed the Reno Ranch, it housed the rambunctious Reno clan and countless wild creatures that they brought in—from an alligator to a boa constrictor to an otter. That house is still Janet Reno's home in Florida.

Janet's mother—outrageous, outspoken, and indifferent to anyone's opinion—taught her children to do the right thing. Janet's sister recalled that growing up, "we had very few rules except that we couldn't do what was wrong. We could be wild, adventurous, enthusiastic about anything we chose. But we couldn't be mean, and we couldn't be dishonest."

Those teachings stuck with Janet, who grew up fast. By the age of 11, she stood 5 feet 11 inches and was taller than everyone in her class, including the teacher. But she didn't seem concerned about it and never walked slumped over.

When Janet was 13, her great uncle, a U.S. military judge, invited her to Germany for a year of schooling. On holidays, she traveled to other coun-

Reno in her Miami law office in 1970.

tries in Europe and fell in love with the sense of history. Back in Florida, she attended Coral Gables High School, was voted "most intelligent" by her senior classmates, and graduated in 1956.

Although Janet had some scholarship money to Cornell University in New York, her parents sold off a chunk of their land to help with college expenses. Janet also worked at college and during summer breaks at the Dade County Sheriff's Office at the courthouse. On her lunch hours, she would sneak into the courtroom, fascinated by the lawyers in action. Her undergraduate degree was in chemistry, but Janet wanted to become a lawyer. She was accepted as one of 16 women in a class of over 500 at Harvard Law School and graduated in 1963.

The love of family and the Everglades' bayous and swamps called Janet Reno home. She passed the Florida bar exam, was hired by a law firm, and joined Miami's chapter of Young Democrats. Working for positive change challenged her, and she volunteered to help Gerald Lewis campaign for a seat in the state legislature. He won his 1966 election, and then he and Janet set up a law office together. Her new partner described her as "one of the best attorneys I've ever known. You've never met a more organized person."

In 1971, Janet Reno launched her public service career. As general counsel for the Florida House of Representatives Judiciary Committee, she revised the constitutional amendment to reform Florida's courts. The amendment was approved by the voters.

Now that she knew more about the political system, Reno decided to try her luck as a candidate. She filed for a vacant state representative seat for Dade County and received valuable advice from friend and politician Jack Orr. "Don't talk out of both sides of your mouth just to be popular. Say what you believe and you will wake up the next morning feeling good about yourself."

Reno defeated a field of Democrats in the primary. At the polls in November 1972, she was defeated by the Republican candidate. But she was not defeated in spirit. "Well, I did not feel exactly good the morning after my election, but I remembered what Jack Orr told me, and that is what I have tried to follow ever since."

The day after her defeat, Dade County state attorney Richard Gerstein offered Reno a job. She had not considered being a prosecutor—that is, prosecuting accused criminals in court—but she was persuaded to take the position. Her first assignment was to set up the Juvenile Division. After three and a half years as a prosecutor, Reno bowed out of public service to practice law as a partner at a prestigious firm. Now she had weekends free, and she filled them with hiking, canoeing, and scuba diving, but allowed time to do pro bono (free) legal work for the poor.

In 1978, her old boss Gerstein resigned from his job, and the governor appointed Janet Reno, 39, as the first woman state attorney in Florida. She filled out the term until the November election, then won the position.

She developed a new routine. Up at six, she'd drink a cup of tea, drive the half hour to the office, and prepare for a 7:30 session with her Spanish tutor. Since many residents of Miami were Spanish-speaking, Reno was determined to communicate easily with them.

She set up the day's agenda, checked on important cases, and often ate lunch at her desk. During the afternoon, she held staff meetings, met with constituents, and returned phone calls. Most days she spoke to a community group to stay in touch with the people she served. If it was a night meeting, she'd sometimes get home after midnight. She kept a sleeping bag at the office for emergencies.

And she needed it. In 1979, five white policemen were charged with beating a black man to death after a high-speed car chase. When a jury found them not guilty, the black community in the Liberty City area of Miami rioted. For four days in May 1980, snipers, mobs, and looters ran wild. Rioters chanted "Reno! Reno! Reno!" Leaders in the black community called for her resignation.

When order was restored, 16 were dead, hundreds were injured, and more than 1,000 were arrested on riot-related charges. Reno defended her office and went into black neighborhoods explaining the trial

Nominated for U.S. attorney general in 1993, Reno is sworn in during her confirmation hearings.

and the prosecutors' case. She went on radio talk shows. She didn't apologize for her office, she just explained and explained.

People listened. Some of her opponents became her supporters. She won reelection in 1980, 1984, 1988, and 1992. She worked against the criminally insane immigrants Castro boated over from Cuba, the crack cocaine epidemic, and street violence. Reno became an advocate for children and came to believe that the first few years of a child's life were crucial to whether that child would later become a criminal.

"She's the hardest-working government official I have ever met," said Tom Cash, an agent for the Drug Enforcement Administration, who worked with her for several years. "She's a person who looks for solutions. She's not one of those who continues to describe the problems."

In Washington, D.C., newly elected president Bill Clinton heard of Reno's accomplishments and added her name to his list of candidates for attorney general. His first two nominees to head the Justice Department had not been well received by the Senate Judiciary Committee, which must approve all cabinet appointees. Reno was invited to Washington for a job interview and a thorough FBI background check.

Clinton liked her immediately and, when he introduced her at a press conference as his nominee for attorney general, said, "She is a front-line crime fighter and a caring public servant. She has devoted her life to making her community safer, keeping children out of trouble, reducing domestic violence, and helping families."

In March 1993, Janet Reno was approved by the Senate committee by a vote of 18–0 and was confirmed by the entire Senate, 98–0. She became the

78th attorney general and the first woman to fill that cabinet post, which oversees nearly 100,000 employees and several agencies: Bureau of Prisons, Federal Bureau of Investigation (FBI), Immigration and Naturalization Service, U.S. Marshals Service, and Community Relations Service.

She inherited many problems when she walked into her office on her first day. Outside of Waco, Texas, FBI agents were in a standoff with a religious cult. The group had stockpiled weapons and killed four agents of the Bureau of Alcohol, Tobacco, and Firearms when they had attempted to serve a search warrant.

Reno testifies before the House Judiciary Committee in April 1993, taking responsibility for the debacle in Waco, Texas–and earning public respect for her courage and honesty.

By mid-April the FBI had a plan to end the siege by using tear gas. Reno asked questions about the tactics and evaluated the answers. Finally, she approved the plan, which was put into action on April 19, 1993. Shortly after noon the cult's compound went up in flames, killing 75 people inside. The fire was set in three places by cult members, but outrage was aimed at the FBI.

At a late afternoon press conference, Reno said, "I made the decisions. I'm accountable. The buck stops with me, and nobody ever accused me of running from a decision that I made based on the best information that I had."

"She stood up and took a bullet for us," an FBI agent said. Her actions earned her loyalty from her own department and a following in the general public.

The press turned her into a folk hero. A government official taking responsibility for her actions instead of placing the blame elsewhere was a rarity. She told reporters not to make her something she wasn't. "I do have a temper. My mother accused me of mumbling. I am not a good housekeeper. My fifth-grade teacher said I was bossy. My family thinks I'm opinionated and sometimes arrogant, and they would be happy to supply you with other words."

Still, her popularity soared and her approval numbers were higher than the president's. She made decisions she felt were the right thing to do, even though they weren't popular with the White House or other government officials. She and the president she served became distant. In her first term as attorney general, she attacked Hollywood for violence on TV that influenced children. She traveled to most of the states, spreading the message of crime prevention. Doing what she considered the right thing to do, she appointed an independent counsel (not a lawyer from the Justice Department) to look into the Whitewater land development scheme that President Clinton had invested in and where legal improprieties had been charged.

After President Clinton was reelected in 1996, he let it be known that he wanted her to resign from his cabinet, but she refused. If he wanted to fire her, he could, but her popularity was still high, and firing her wasn't the politically expedient thing to do. She stayed on as attorney general.

Once asked if she considered herself the president's attorney or the people's attorney, she answered without hesitation, "The people's attorney."

Walter Dellinger, who had worked for Reno and now teaches law at Duke University, summed up Reno's character. "She simply does not respond to the system of positive and negative incentives that works in Washington: fear of criticism and ambition for higher office." He sees her as "the single most inner-directed person I have ever known, without a doubt."

When her time as the head of the Justice Department is over, Reno plans to return to her rustic home on the edge of the swamp and continue to do what she feels is the right thing to do.

MADELEINE ALBRIGHT

6

As a competent negotiator, she left nothing to chance. Even before December 1996, when President Bill Clinton nominated United Nations ambassador Madeleine Albright as secretary of state, she had begun courting members of the Senate Judiciary Committee, who would be conducting confirmation hearings. She convinced them she was qualified for the job. After her nomination, she went door to door to meet other senators, because they had the final vote. She watched the Senate voting proceedings on television in her office in New York at the United Nations. When the tally was announced, 99–0, she fell back in her chair and whooped. She was secretary of state, the highest office a woman has ever held in American government.

It was a job she had prepared for all her life.

Marie Jana Korbelova (soon changed to Madeleine Korbel) was born on May 15, 1937, the oldest daughter of Josef and Anna, in Prague, Czechoslovakia. Her father was a diplomat, and Madeleine's first lesson in foreign affairs was as a youngster, when she dressed in national costume to present flowers to dignitaries.

Madeleine Albright on her first day in office as secretary of state.

55

In 1938, Hitler's Nazis overran her country, and her family fled to London. Here she learned to speak English. Her memories of World War II centered around a newly invented steel table. "If your house was bombed and you were under the table, you would survive. We ate on the table, slept under the table, and played around the table."

At the end of the war, her family returned to Czechoslovakia and later moved to Belgrade, Yugoslavia, where her father served as the Czech ambassador. She was taught by a governess because her father didn't want her exposed to communism in Yugoslavian schools. At age 10, she attended boarding school in Switzerland, where she learned to speak French.

"I made friends very easily," she said. "I think it has to do with the fact that I lived in a lot of different countries, went to a lot of different schools, and was always being put into situations where I had to relate to the people around me."

In 1948, her father represented Czechoslovakia on the U.N. Commission for India and Pakistan. Madeleine and her younger sister and brother accompanied their parents to New York. During this time, the Czech government was overthrown by Communists, and her father learned that while he was away he had been charged as a traitor and sentenced to death. The Korbel family was granted political asylum in the United States.

They moved to Colorado, where Josef Korbel taught at the University of Denver and later became dean of the Graduate School of International Studies. He and his wife raised their children as Catholics, and as a new citizen, Madeleine worked at losing her foreign accent and becoming Americanized. On scholarship, she attended a small private high school and graduated in 1955. Also on scholarship, she attended prestigious Wellesley College in Massachusetts, majoring in political science, but dabbling in journalism. At a summer job with the *Denver Post,* she met newspaper heir Joseph Albright. A few days after she graduated from Wellesley with honors in 1959, they were married and settled in Chicago.

In 1961, they moved to New York, and Madeleine Albright gave birth to premature twins, Alice and Anne. While they remained in incubators for nearly two months, she took an eight-hour-a-day course in Russian to take her mind off her anxiety. After her daughters were home and thriving, she enrolled in graduate school in public law and government at Columbia University. She continued in school after the birth of a third daughter, Katie, and studied by getting up at 4:30 and squeezing in time around family activities. By the time the family moved to Washington, D.C, in 1968, she had earned her master's degree and was doing final work on her doctoral dissertation.

On the board of directors of her twins' school, Albright was assigned the task of soliciting donations. She had never raised money before, but she was good at it, and another parent at the school asked her to cochair a fund-raiser for Senator Edmund Muskie. "That's how the whole thing started," Albright said. When she finished her doctorate, she took a job as Muskie's chief legislative assistant. He was on the Senate Foreign Relations Committee, and Albright spent a lot of time dealing with foreign affairs.

In 1978, Albright was hired by a former teacher at Columbia to work for the National Security Council while Democrat Jimmy Carter was president. When the Republicans took over the White House in 1981, Albright was temporarily out of a job.

Albright's experience at the United Nations prepared her for dealing with world leaders like Yasser Arafat.

After the breakup of her marriage in 1982, Madeleine Albright looked for new direction in her life. She was hired by two research institutes and taught international affairs at Georgetown University. For four years straight, students voted her best professor in the School of Foreign Service. In the evenings she would invite influential Democrats to her home, where the food was not exactly gourmet, but the foreign policy conversations were stimulating. As one frequent guest said, "You did not go to Madeleine's for the food. You went for the discussion."

Albright served as foreign policy adviser for Geraldine Ferraro during the 1984 vice presidential campaign and for Michael Dukakis during his bid for president in 1988. She met Arkansas Governor Bill Clinton when he went to Boston to help Dukakis prepare for debates, and they kept in touch.

When Clinton was elected president in 1992 and promised a cabinet that would "look like America,"

Albright was an easy choice for ambassador to the United Nations.

As the U.S. ambassador, she was the only woman who served on the U.N. Security Council. She visited the home countries of the other 14 council members and made trips to numerous foreign capitals that weren't important enough to merit a visit from the secretary of state. She dropped in on military posts abroad to learn firsthand about their peace-keeping missions.

And she went on television. Keeping Americans interested in the United States' foreign policy during peacetime was a task she was willing to take on. Because she could put complex issues into simple language that the average citizen could understand, she became a Clinton spokeswoman for foreign policy.

Her position at the United Nations also gave her cabinet rank, and she shuttled between Washington and New York. At times she'd get off the 6:00 morning shuttle at the New York airport and her beeper would inform her she was needed back in Washington for a meeting of the National Security Council. She'd immediately climb back on the shuttle for the return trip.

She didn't have time to waste, so she didn't join the U.N. social circuit. "I don't go to receptions. I sometimes think I came up here [to the United Nations in New York] to eat for my country, but they are not my cup of tea." She was frank and outspoken, and she worked hard, doing her homework on each issue that came before the United Nations.

"I have always believed—and I say this to my daughters, and I said it to my students—whatever the job you are asked to do at whatever level, do a good job because your reputation is your resume."

When Clinton was reelected for a second term in

Albright lays a small stone on the tomb of assassinated Israeli prime minister Yitzhak Rabin in 1997. Her own family's background gives her a special understanding of war and political turmoil.

The secretary of state holds a young child during a visit to Guatemala.

1996 and Warren Christopher decided he would step down as secretary of state, a search was on for his replacement. Many names were mentioned as candidates, but Madeleine Albright's name appeared on everyone's list. Her time at the United Nations was the final training ground for the State Department's biggest job.

After Clinton had named her as the first woman secretary of state and she had been confirmed by the Senate, Madeleine Albright discovered more about her roots in Czechoslovakia. Three of her grandparents had died in the Jewish Holocaust in World War II, but her parents had never told her of her Jewish origins. She felt that her parents' decision to flee their country had saved her life.

"I have been very proud of who I am and the values that my parents taught me," she said, "and as I now find out more about my heritage, obviously I'm very proud of it."

Ever since Albright had become an international figure, she had been getting letters from people in Prague who had known her family. So when a reporter researched her family's history, using documents recently made available in the Czech Republic, and published his findings about her Jewish roots, he didn't catch her totally unprepared. "What I was surprised about was that my grandparents died in concentration camps."

As a two-time refugee, Albright looks on America with gratitude and spreads that feeling around the globe. She visited 52 countries in 1997, more than any other secretary of state in the first year of office. In November of that year, she stopped at a girls' school at an Afghan refugee camp in Pakistan and told the young Muslim girls about her past. She knelt on their level to say goodbye. "We really all are sisters," she said. "I will never forget you."

As an advocate for human rights and democratic principles, Albright has dedicated her stint as secretary of state to the good the United States can do in the world.

"I have been privileged to live my life in freedom," she has said. "Millions have still never had that opportunity. . . . It is not enough for us to say that Communism has failed. We too must heed the lessons of the past, accept responsibility, and lead."

CHRONOLOGY

1916   Republican Jeannette Rankin of Montana is the first woman elected to the U.S. House of Representatives.

1920   Women vote in a national election for the first time.

1925   Nellie Tayloe Ross of Wyoming becomes the first woman state governor, succeeding her husband, who died in office.

1932   Hattie Wyatt Caraway is the first woman elected to the U.S. Senate. She had earlier been appointed to complete her late husband's term.

1933   Frances Perkins, the first woman to hold a cabinet post, is named secretary of labor by President Franklin D. Roosevelt.

1949   Eugenie Moore Anderson becomes the first woman U.S. ambassador, representing the country in Denmark.

1968   Shirley Chisholm of New York becomes the first black woman elected to the U.S. House of Representatives.

1972   Barbara Jordan of Texas becomes the first black woman from the South to be elected to the U.S. House of Representatives.

1981   Sandra Day O'Connor, the first woman on the Supreme Court, is appointed by President Ronald Reagan and confirmed by the Senate.

1984   Geraldine Ferraro (Democrat) becomes the first woman vice presidential candidate nominated by a major party.

1992   Carol Moseley-Braun becomes the first black woman elected to the U.S. Senate.

1993   Janet Reno, the first woman attorney general, is appointed by President Bill Clinton and confirmed by the Senate.

1997   Madeleine Albright, the first woman secretary of state, is confirmed by the Senate after her appointment by President Bill Clinton.

FURTHER READING

Blue, Rose, and Corinne Naden. *Barbara Jordan*. Philadelphia: Chelsea House, 1992.

Byman, Jeremy. *Madame Secretary: Story of Madeleine Albright*. Greensboro, N.C.: Morgan Reynolds, 1997.

Carrigan, Mellonee. *Carol Moseley-Braun: Breaking Barriers*. Chicago: Children's Press, 1994.

Ferraro, Geraldine, with Linda Bird Francke. *Ferraro: My Story*. New York: Bantam, 1985.

Freedman, Suzanne. *Madeleine Albright: She Speaks for America*. Danbury, Conn.: Franklin Watts, 1998.

Herda, D. J. *Sandra Day O'Connor: Independent Thinker*. Springfield, N.J.: Enslow, 1995.

Huber, Peter. *Sandra Day O'Connor*. Philadelphia: Chelsea House, 1990.

Jeffrey, Laura S. *Barbara Jordan: Congresswoman, Lawyer, Educator*. Springfield, N.J.: Enslow, 1997.

Jordan, Barbara, and Shelby Hearon. *Barbara Jordan, A Self-Portrait*. Garden City, N.Y.: Doubleday, 1979.

Lawson, Don. *Geraldine Ferraro: The Woman Who Changed American Politics, July 16, 1998*. New York: Messner, 1985.

Meachum, Virginia. *Janet Reno: United States Attorney General*. Springfield, N.J.: Enslow, 1995.

Simon, Charnan. *Janet Reno: First Woman Attorney General*. San Francisco: Children's Book Press, 1994.

INDEX

ABOUT THE AUTHOR

Award-winning writer Veda Boyd Jones enjoys the challenge of writing for a variety of readers. Her published works include nine adult novels, three children's historical novels, three children's biographies, a coloring book, and numerous articles and short stories in national magazines. Jones holds a master's degree in history from the University of Arkansas; she teaches writing and speaks at writers' conferences. She lives in Missouri with her husband, Jimmie, and three sons, Landon, Morgan, and Marshall.